Be the Best

VOLLEYBALL

A Step-By-Step Guide

By Charles Bracken

Troll Associates

Library of Congress Cataloging-in-Publication Data

Bracken, Charles.
    Volleyball, a step-by-step guide / by Charles Bracken.
      p.   cm.—(Be the best!)
    Summary: Examines the equipment, skills, and rules associated with
volleyball.
    ISBN 0-8167-1951-9 (lib. bdg.)   ISBN 0-8167-1952-7 (pbk.)
    1. Volleyball—Juvenile literature. [1. Volleyball.] I. Title.
II. Series.
GV1015.3.B73 1990
796.325—dc20   89-27352

Be the Best

VOLLEYBALL

A Step-By-Step Guide

FOREWORD

by Bob Gambardella

Volleyball, A Step-by-Step Guide, is a great book for a young person to learn about the sport. It teaches all the skills you'll need to get started.

Once you've read this book, share your volleyball knowledge with all your friends. Then try to get some teams together to play. There's plenty of fun and excitement in volleyball—enough to last a lifetime!

Robert Gambardella

Bob Gambardella is the head volleyball coach at the United States Military Academy in West Point, New York. He has been head coach there since 1983. In the past, Bob has served as a board member of the American Volleyball Coaches Association. And in 1989, he was volleyball commissioner at the U.S. Olympic Festival held in Oklahoma City, Oklahoma.

Contents

Volleyball— Fun for Everyone

Enjoyed all over the world, volleyball is an inexpensive, fun sport. It can be played indoors or outdoors. Volleyball can be a serious, competitive sport or a game played just for fun without paying strict attention to the rules. One reason volleyball is so popular is that it is basically a very simple game. All you really have to do is hit a ball back and forth over a net and keep the ball from touching the ground on your side.

Another reason for volleyball's popularity is that almost anyone can play the game and play it fairly well with just a little practice. You don't have to be tall, strong, or fast to play volleyball. Volleyball players come in all shapes, sizes, and ages.

Because volleyball doesn't need much special equipment, it is a perfect game to play at the beach, at a picnic, or in a gym during winter. So whatever the season is, you can always enjoy the game of volleyball.

The Story of Volleyball

Volleyball is a much older game than many people believe. The sport is an adaptation of an old Italian game that originated way back in the Middle Ages. Around the mid-1890s, the Italian game spread to nearby Germany where it was called *faustball*.

Faustball was played on a rectangular court divided down the middle by a rope suspended above the floor. There were five players on each side of the rope. The object was to hit a ball over the rope. In this game, it was legal to hit a ball even after it bounced twice off the floor.

In 1895, at a YMCA in Holyoke, Massachusetts, an instructor named William G. Morgan invented his own special version of *faustball*. He called it "mintonette." It was an indoor game meant to keep adults fit without too much physical exertion. Morgan hung a tennis net above the gymnasium floor, and he used the inflated inside bladder of a basketball for a ball.

FAUSTBALL–1890

The rules of Morgan's new game were simple. Teams stood on opposite sides of the net. They volleyed a ball back and forth over the net. The ball had to be kept up in the air and could not be played off the floor. If one team allowed the ball to hit the ground, the opposing team scored a point.

Eventually, "mintonette" spread throughout New England. And when a college instructor named Alfred T. Halstead watched a game, he suggested the name be changed to "volleyball." It has been known by that name ever since. William Morgan, however, is still considered the Father of Volleyball because the game he developed is almost identical to the modern game.

FIRST VOLLEYBALL CHAMPIONSHIPS 1929

As the years passed, volleyball grew more and more popular in America. In 1897, the sport's first official rules were printed. That same year, the first national volleyball tournament was held. In 1928, the United States Volleyball Association was founded. Soon afterward, it held its first championships.

American soldiers fighting in foreign countries during World War I and especially during World War II helped spread the game of volleyball overseas. Shortly after the Second World War, in 1947, the International Volleyball Federation was formed. And the U.S. Volleyball Association became one of its thirteen charter members.

In 1964, another important milestone was achieved. Volleyball was finally accepted as an Olympic sport. Today, it is a favorite of men and women, and boys and girls, all over the world.

What You Need To Play Volleyball

Volleyball is a game that uses very little special equipment. All you really need to play are a level, flat area (indoors or outdoors), a net suspended above the ground or floor, a medium-sized ball, and some friends.

UNIFORMS

There really is no such thing as a special volleyball uniform. Most teams in competition wear shorts, numbered T-shirts, and sneakers. Many volleyball uniforms look very much like basketball uniforms.

VOLLEYBALL UNIFORMS

Elbow Pads

Knee-pads

Shorts

Sweat Pants

Players who wear shorts and sleeveless shirts sometimes wear elbow pads and kneepads for extra protection, especially for indoor play. Sometimes volleyball players dive on the ground for balls, and these protective pads help them avoid bruises and skin scrapes.

For informal volleyball games, players wear just about anything. Loose-fitting shirts and jeans or sweat pants are fine. For beach volleyball, some players prefer to go barefoot. What you wear for a volleyball game isn't really that important as long as your clothing doesn't restrict your movement.

VOLLEYBALL

Air Pressure 7 Pounds

Weighs 9-10 Ounces

THE VOLLEYBALL

A volleyball is a medium-sized ball made of leather or rubber. It is inflated to an air pressure of about seven pounds. The ball is twenty-five to twenty-seven inches all the way around and weighs nine to ten ounces.

VOLLEYBALL COURT

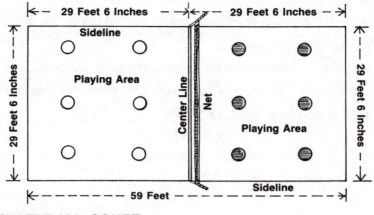

VOLLEYBALL COURT

A volleyball court is rectangular. It measures fifty-nine feet long and twenty-nine and a half feet wide. The boundary lines around the court (painted lines) are two inches wide. The long lines on the court are called the *sidelines*. The lines at the back of the court are called the *end lines.*

The court is divided by a *center line* across the middle of the court. The center line separates the court into two playing areas that measure twenty-nine and a half by twenty-nine and a half feet.

A net is hung above and along the center line. For students in grades one through six, the top of the net is six feet one inch above the floor. Grades seven through nine play with a net seven feet four and one-eighth inches above the floor. The net itself is three feet wide and thirty-two feet long.

VOLLEYBALL TEAM

For an unofficial volleyball game, two players or more can play on one side. In official volleyball games, however, only six players per team are allowed to be on the court at one time.

The way players on each team are usually positioned is three in the front near the net and three in the back near the end line (see page 18).

How to Play Volleyball

At the start of a volleyball game, the six players on each team must position themselves in two rows of three. The front three are near the net. From left to right, they are called the left front, the center front, and the right front. The back three are near the end line. From left to right, they are called the left back, the center back, and the right back. All of the team players stand an equal distance apart so that the entire playing area on their side of the net is well covered. Each player tries to stay in a specific area during play. Except for special plays, players *do not* run all over the court or bunch up.

VOLLEYBALL COURT AND PLAYERS

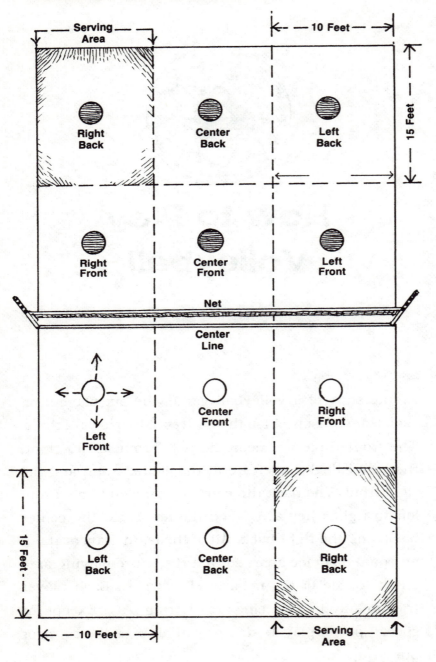

To begin the game, the ball must be put into play. A flip of the coin usually decides which team will put the ball in play first. Play begins with a *serve*. Only one player on a team serves the ball at a time. Whether you are serving is determined by where you are on the court. The server is always the right back or the player positioned in the back row and to the right of the court facing the net. You will later see that players change positions several times during a game so that the same person does not serve throughout the contest.

PLAYER SERVING

To serve, a player takes the ball and stands with both feet behind the end line and to the right side of the court. That is the *serving area*. Using only *one hand*, the server then hits the ball over the net into the opposing team's court.

A serve is no good if the ball touches the server's court, a player on the server's team, or the net. If the serve goes under the net or out of bounds, it is also no good. A player only gets one chance to make a good serve. If the serve is not good, the ball goes to the opposing team. It's now their turn to serve.

Once the ball legally passes over the net on a good serve, it must be volleyed back and forth over the net. During this volleying, the ball may be hit with one or two hands. The object is not to let the ball touch the floor on your side of the court. The *serving team* scores a point if the ball touches the opposing team's court or if the opposing team hits the ball out of bounds. If the serving team scores a point, the player who served the last point serves again.

If the serving team allows the ball to hit their side of the court, hits the ball out of bounds, or makes a bad

serve, the opposition *does not* score a point. Points can only be scored by the team serving the ball. If the serving team commits an error, that is called a *side out*. Neither team scores a point on a side out. But the opposing team does win the serve and with it the chance to score points on their own. Again, *only* the serving team can score points.

A volleyball match for young players is no more than three games long. A team has to win two games to win the match. And if a team wins the first two games of a match, it's over and that team wins it.

A volleyball game is won by the first team to score fifteen points with a victory margin of at least two points. A team cannot win a game by the score of 15 to 14, for example. It would take a score of at least 16 to 14 to win that game. No matter how long a game is played, it continues until that two-point victory margin is achieved.

Another interesting part of volleyball is that every player eventually gets a chance to serve. Every time a team wins back a serve after a side out, the players *rotate* their positions clockwise. If a team does not rotate, the serve is illegal.

To rotate legally, the players in the back move one position to the left. The left back at the far left moves up to the front line to become the left front. The players in the front line move one position to the right. The right front moves into the back line to become the right back or server. The rotation must be done every time a team gets to serve after a side out.

VOLLEYBALL ROTATION
AFTER A SIDE OUT

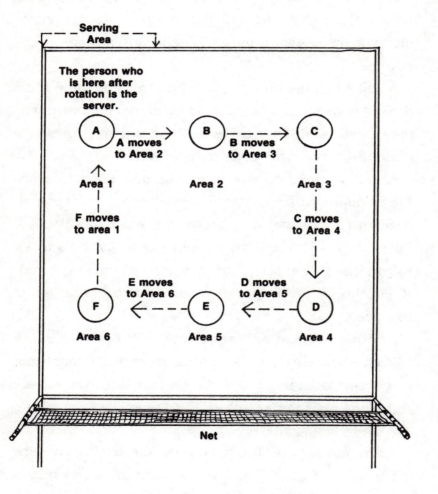

While you're volleying during a game, there are other simple rules you should keep in mind. You are not allowed to grasp or hold the ball before returning it. Throwing the ball instead of hitting it is also illegal. On a ball near the top of the net, you are not allowed to reach over the net to hit the ball or to touch the net.

EACH TEAM IS ALLOWED TO HIT THE BALL THREE TIMES

Hit #1   Hit #2   Hit #3

During play, each team is allowed to hit the ball three times on their side of the net. The same player, however, is not allowed to hit the ball two times in a row. But it *is* legal for a player to hit the ball the first and third times as long as someone else on the team hits it the second time. Good volleyball teams always try to use all three hits in order to make a good attack when they hit the ball over the net to the other team.

Serving

Serving is one of the most important parts of volleyball and one of the most important skills to learn. Without proper serves, a team cannot score any points. Remember that you get only one chance to make a serve good. When serving, keep your eyes on the ball and concentrate.

As we discussed on page 19, all serves must be made from the serving area. And you can only use one hand to serve.

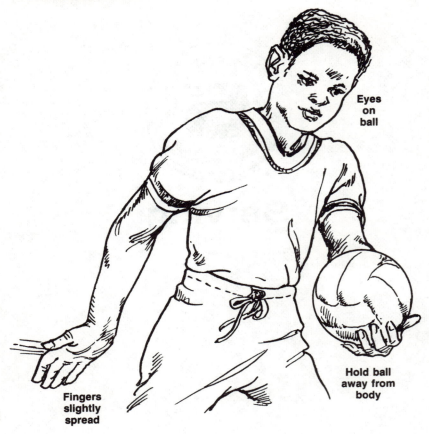

Eyes
on
ball

Hold ball
away from
body

Fingers
slightly
spread

UNDERHAND SERVE

The underhand serve is the best serve for beginners. It is a straight serve with an upward arch that usually clears the net. An underhand serve is also accurate and easy to control.

The explanation that follows is for a right-handed server. If you're a left-handed server, reverse the hand and foot positions described here.

OPEN-PALM UNDERHAND SERVE

1.

Hand under ball

2.

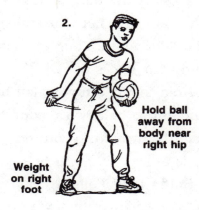

Hold ball away from body near right hip

Weight on right foot

Trunk leans forward as arm swings back, then forward

3.

Eyes on ball

Fingers slightly spread

4.

5.

Toss the ball and strike the middle of the underside

6.

Follow through

To start an underhand serve, stand in the serving area and face the net. Your feet should be spread about shoulder width. Your left foot should be slightly forward and your knees bent.

Hold the ball in your left hand. Your hand should be *under* the ball, with your fingertips pointed up and slightly away from your body. Keep your fingers spread wide apart. That will help you control the ball better.

Hold the ball slightly out from your body so it is just outside and in front of your right hip. Your weight should be mostly on your right foot. Lean your trunk forward as you swing your right arm up behind you. Keep your eyes on the ball and concentrate!

Keep the fingers of your right hand only slightly spread. You want to hit the ball with the palm of your hand. Toss the ball up with your left hand and strike it near the middle of the underside. You have to hit the ball hard enough to clear the net but not so hard that it will go out of bounds. Hitting the ball off center may also cause it to go out of bounds to the side.

Keep your right hand and wrist stiff as you hit the ball. When your hand makes contact, shift your weight forward from your right foot to your left foot. Follow through by allowing your right arm to continue to swing outward and upward.

FOLLOW THROUGH

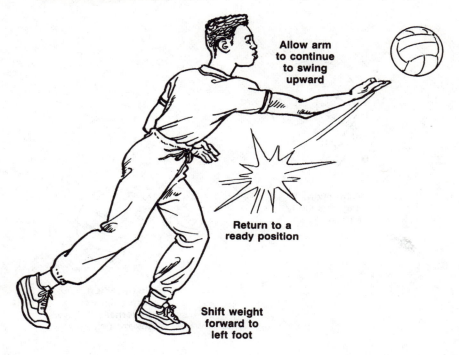

Allow arm
to continue
to swing
upward

Return to a
ready position

Shift weight
forward to
left foot

UNDERHAND SERVE VARIATIONS

Once you master the open-palm underhand serve, you may want to try a few variations. You do them by changing the position of your striking hand. They can make your underhand serve tougher to return.

Some of the more popular variations of the underhand serve follow.

Using a Fist Instead of keeping your palm open, curl your fingers into a fist. Hitting the ball with your fist will make your serve harder and faster. However, it may also hurt your accuracy.

HAND POSITIONS FOR UNDERHAND SERVE

A. Palm open,
   fingers slightly
   spread

B. Fist position
   with palm up;
   fingernails
   toward ball

You can keep your hand in the same position as described earlier for an underhand serve, This time, however, curl your fingers into a fist. Then strike the ball with the knuckles of your fingers.

Sidearm Serve   In this variation of the underhand serve, your body should be positioned as it would for a regular underhand serve. The difference is in the swing of your striking arm. Bend your arm more at the elbow. And instead of bringing your arm forward in an underhand motion, move it forward out to the side. Your striking hand can be open or a fist. Generally, this is not a good serve for beginners. It is, however, a hard and fast serve.

SIDEARM SERVE

Arm swing is out to side and forward from side

Regular swing is straight back, then forward

Spin   Putting spin on the ball can make returning your serve both tricky and difficult. However, beginners who try to make the ball curve by putting spin on their serve may end up with a side out. Getting the ball to spin just right is not easy and takes lots of practice.

OUTCURVE SPIN SERVE

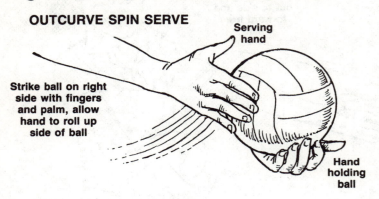

Serving hand

Strike ball on right side with fingers and palm, allow hand to roll up side of ball

Hand holding ball

To make the ball spin to your left as it crosses the net (which is sometimes called an *outcurve*), do not strike the ball in the center and a little underneath with your hand as usual. Instead, hit the ball on the right side, using your fingers and palm more than the heel of your hand. As you strike the ball, let your hand roll up the ball's side and over the top. That is what makes the ball spin and curve.

Floater   This is another tricky serve. It is like a baseball pitcher's knuckleball. A floater sails through the air with little or no spin. It is a tough serve to handle and even tougher to do correctly.

For a floater, curl your fingers into a half-fist. Bend your fingers at the first two joints so that the tips are over your palm but not resting against it. Bend your thumb in so

A FLOATER

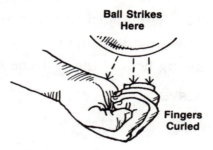

Ball Strikes Here

Fingers Curled

its tip touches the tip of your first finger. When you hit the ball, strike it with your fingernails, knuckles, and heel of your hand. Do not hit it with the flat of your palm.

OVERHAND SERVE

The overhand serve is the best and most powerful serve in volleyball. However, it can be difficult for beginners to learn and master. It is best to stick with the underhand serve until you can do it fairly well. Only then should you try to move on to the overhand serve.

TOSS UP FOR OVERHAND SERVE

Ball should be halfway between arm and face

The explanation that follows is for a right-handed server. If you're a left-handed server, reverse the hand and foot positions described here.

Start by standing behind the end line in the serving

OVERHAND SERVE

1.

Face net

Ball held at chest level

Knees bent

Right foot behind body

Foot behind end line

2. Left hand behind ear

Eyes on ball

Toss ball up in front of face

Feet shoulder width apart

3. Arm comes forward

Time your hit

Rise up on toes to meet ball

4. Hit ball dead center

Strike ball at a point a foot above head

Turn torso to left

Shift weight forward

area. Face the net and keep your knees slightly bent. Place your left foot about six to twelve inches behind the end line. Turn your hips to the right a bit and place your right foot back behind you. Your feet should be about shoulder width apart. Your weight should be on your right or back foot.

Hold the ball in your left hand just as you did for an underhand serve (see page 26). But hold the ball up higher, about chest level. Draw your right hand up behind your ear as if you were about to throw something. The palm of your right hand should face the net and your fingers should be together or slightly spread, whichever you prefer.

Keeping your eyes trained on the ball, toss the ball up out of your left hand in front of your face. The ball should be about half the distance of your fully outstretched left arm from your face. The ball should also rise about twenty to thirty inches above eye level.

As the ball goes up, your weight should be on your back foot. Bend your torso slightly backward as you begin the swing of your right arm forward. It is an overhand swing like a baseball pitcher's throw or a service swing in tennis.

Rise up on your toes to meet the ball as it comes down. Move your arm forward in a whiplike fashion as you keep your eyes trained on the ball. Be sure to time your hit. You should strike the ball when it reaches a level just above your head. Hit the ball dead center with the palm of your hand. Keep your wrist stiff as you strike the ball.

As you hit the ball, get your body into the serve. Shift your weight forward to the left foot and turn your torso to the left. Follow through by allowing your arm to continue in a circular motion forward and by taking a step forward with your back foot.

PLACING SERVES

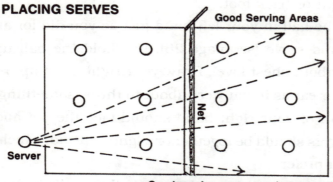

Good serving areas are: between players, near end lines, or near sidelines.

PLACING A SERVE

The first concern of all beginning servers should be just to get the ball over the net and in bounds. However, once you become better and better at serving, you can make an effort to place your serve. That means you hit the ball to a specific area you want it to go to.

A good rule of thumb in placing a serve is to try to hit the ball between two opposing players rather than hitting the ball directly at any one player.

Another good idea is to keep your serves high enough to go over the front line. Try to serve to the backcourt just inside the end line. It is also best to serve to the right or left of the court rather than the middle area where the opposition has a better chance to return the ball.

Hitting and Returning

The real fun of a volleyball game is being able to volley the ball back and forth over the net several times in a row. And that takes good eye-hand coordination as well as skill. In other words, a player's eyes and hands must work well together. Keeping your eyes on the ball as it comes toward you and timing your hand contact with the ball just right will normally get the ball back over the net.

OVERHAND RETURN

An easy way to get the ball back over the net is to use an overhand return. This type of hit takes two hands to do and works best when the ball is hit right to you or very close to you.

To hit the ball with two hands, you should be facing the net with your feet spread shoulder width apart. Keep your knees bent slightly. Your hands should be held at the level of your forehead and about six inches away from your body. Keep your palms up so that your fingers point toward the ceiling. Your wrists should be bent back and your fingers spread. Your hands should be far enough apart so that if you stretch your fingers out to the sides, they will not touch. Your thumbs should be in and your elbows out to the sides.

OVERHAND RETURN

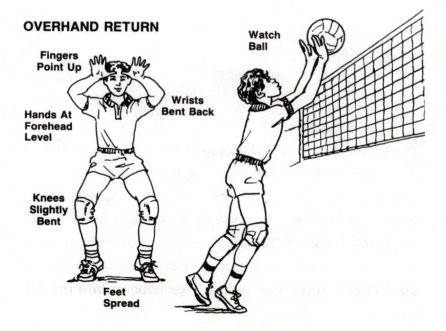

Fingers Point Up

Hands At Forehead Level

Knees Slightly Bent

Feet Spread

Wrists Bent Back

Watch Ball

OVERHAND RETURN

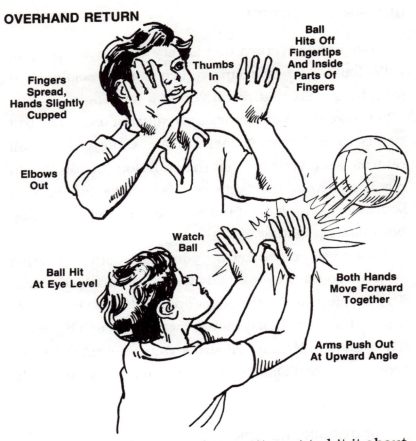

Fingers
Spread,
Hands Slightly
Cupped

Thumbs
In

Ball
Hits Off
Fingertips
And Inside
Parts Of
Fingers

Elbows
Out

Watch
Ball

Ball Hit
At Eye Level

Both Hands
Move Forward
Together

Arms Push Out
At Upward Angle

As the ball comes toward you, attempt to hit it about eye level. Move both your hands forward at the same time. It's like pushing someone away from you. However, do not thrust your arms straight out. They must move outward at an upward angle to give the ball the arch it needs to clear the net.

Watch the ball at all times. Strike it with the fingers of both your hands at the same time. Straighten your flexed knees as you hit the ball, and push off with your feet. This "mini-jump" will get your body into the hit.

UNDERHAND RETURN

A two-handed return that is very often used today in volleyball is an underhand return. It is especially good for hitting balls that reach you at a low angle.

In this return, your hands are really not used. The ball strikes your forearms instead. As is the case on all returns, keep your eyes on the ball. Both hands should reach out from the body as if to shake hands with someone. Keeping the thumbs on top and together, clasp both hands together.

As the ball comes toward you, keep both your arms stretched out from your body with your hands together. To get your arms in the proper position, dip your hands toward the floor so that they are waist high or a bit lower. The idea is to let the ball strike your forearms near the wrists. The ball should hit your arms, not your hands.

UNDERHAND RETURN

Arms
Stretched
Out

Thumbs
On Top

Hands
Clasped
Together

Allow the ball to hit your forearms. Keep your arm swing toward the ball as short as you can. It takes practice to do this correctly, so don't worry if you don't get the technique right the first few times.

Very Little
Or No
Upswing

Allow Ball To Hit
Your Arms And
Bounce Off

Ball
Strikes Here

SPIKE

One of the most aggressive shots in volleyball is the spike. It is exciting to watch. A spike is a powerful one-hand shot that is quite often unreturnable. When it lands inbounds and can't be returned, a "kill" results. Every team wants as many "kills" as they can get. Points pile up fast that way.

In a spike, a player close to the net usually jumps high in the air and slams the ball sharply downward toward the floor on the opposing team's side. But the spike is not just a sudden explosion of strength and power. It is normally aimed at an opening between players. In spiking the ball, a player needs split-second timing, a good eye, upper-body strength, and strong legs for leaping.

The first part of a spike is getting to the ball while it is high above the net. That requires powerful legs. Your jump must be straight up so that you do not touch the net. Doing so will make your shot illegal. Remember, the higher above the net you go, the sharper the angle of your spike can be. So when you jump, first coil your legs by bending at the knees and then spring upward by pushing off with your toes.

Your arm swing for the spike can be done one of two ways. You can use a long, full swing, keeping your arm fully extended. Or you can use a short swing, keeping your elbow bent. Using the bent-elbow swing gets more of the forearm and wrist into the stroke and provides power, but it shortens your reach.

You want to hit the ball just above the middle. Your hand should go up over the ball and come down on it.

The way to position your hand for a spike is to keep your hand open, spreading the fingers wide. The ball is hit with the heel of the hand. Upon contact, snap your hand downward at the wrist. Spiking in this way gives you more control over your shot and makes it much more accurate.

SPIKING

When in the air near the net, keep your other arm close to your body. That will prevent you from touching the net with your free hand.

After hitting the ball, you must maintain good body control in the air. Make sure that the follow-through of your hitting arm doesn't let it touch the net. After you come down, quickly get back to a ready position in case your spike is returned.

Smash Ball Down

Keep Body Control Don't Touch Net

Return To A Ready Position

5.

6.

7.

HAND POSITION FOR SPIKING

Hit Ball With Heel Of Hand

DINK

The spike is volleyball's most powerful shot. The dink, or tip, is just the opposite. It is a very soft, tricky shot meant to catch your opponent off guard and out of position. Deception is the key to a successful dink. This shot is much like a baseball pitcher's change-up pitch.

THE DINK

The dink is done when a ball is near the net. The trick is to go up as if you are going to spike the ball hard. Your body motions have to look just like a spike. However, instead of blasting the ball downward with all your might, you just gently tap it over the net. You do this with your fingers, slapping at the ball with a flick of your wrist. You want the ball to drop straight down quickly on the opposing team's court very near the net.

The dink is usually successful because opposing players are tricked into thinking a spike is coming and so they tend to back up to prepare for it.

BLOCKING THE SPIKE

Blocking begins when one or more front row defensive players jump into the air on the side of the net opposite a spiker. They try to keep the spike from going into their court by having it deflect off their hands back into the spiker's court. Blockers use their hands like a barrier to cut off the path of the spike and change its direction while it's above the net.

Blocking a spike takes good timing. It means being in the right place at the right time. A blocker must jump almost exactly at the same moment the spiker jumps. Anticipating a spike and knowing when to jump are the first steps to a good block. After you play volleyball a while, you will be able to tell when a spike is coming and be able to prepare for it.

BLOCKING THE SPIKE

Both Hands High Over Head

Time Your Jump To Block A Spike

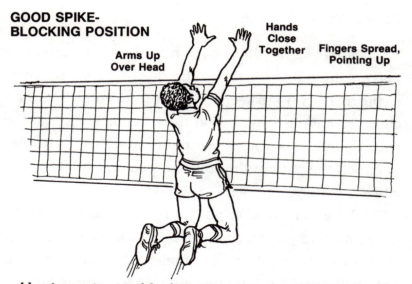

GOOD SPIKE-BLOCKING POSITION

Arms Up Over Head

Hands Close Together

Fingers Spread, Pointing Up

Also important to blocking a spike is your body position in the air. Blocking is done by holding both your hands high in the air over your head and in front of you. Your palms should be toward the net. Your hands should be about three or four inches apart and your fingers spread wide. Hold your hands straight up and down, too. If you hold your hands slightly forward during a block, the ball may trickle down on your side of the net in front of you. If your hands are angled backward, the ball will deflect behind you instead of back into the opposing team's court.

When attempting to block, keep your eyes on the ball. You must try to get your hands in a direct line with the ball's path. Try to get to the ball before it can travel too far on its downward path. That is why timing your jump with the spiker's jump is so important. If your timing is off, the ball may end up in the net on your side or deflect off you and hit your side of the court.

Passing and Setting Up

Remember, the rules of volleyball allow a team to hit the ball three times on their side of the net. A good volleyball team uses those three hits to move the ball around their side of the court and to make an attack. Usually, the shot a team tries to set up is a spike (see page 42).

You'll now learn about different ways to pass the ball in order to set up a teammate for a spike.

OVERHAND PASS

The overhand pass is the most frequently used pass in volleyball and is really quite simple. It is a two-handed pass in which you push the ball forward and upward by thrusting your arms out to meet the ball.

PASSING THE BALL

As the ball approaches, keep your feet spread and your knees bent. Your weight should be on the balls of your feet. Hold your hands up near your forehead. Your arms should be apart and your elbows out. Spread your fingers and point your thumbs downward and a bit forward.

As the ball approaches, bring your arms back toward you and coil them like a spring. As your hands move forward to meet the ball, keep your wrists and fingers stiff. Make contact with the ball with your fingers only, and try to get all ten fingers on it. That will give you control of the ball and slow any spin on it.

Now push the ball away from you by using your fingertips and a wrist snap. Your wrists and fingers are the primary driving force, but make sure you get your arms and body into the pass, too.

Pass the ball away from you at an upward angle. Do not just hit the ball blindly. Send your pass to a teammate. If you are in the back line, send the ball to the front row.

On balls hit low, crouch down or drop to one knee to make an overhand pass.

OVERHAND PASS

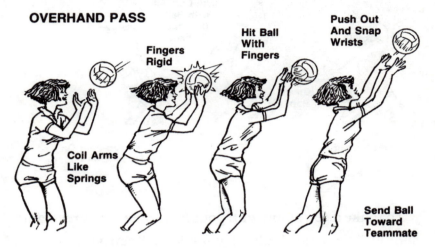

Fingers Rigid

Hit Ball With Fingers

Push Out And Snap Wrists

Coil Arms Like Springs

Send Ball Toward Teammate

THE SET

A set comes after someone on your team has already passed the ball once. The set is the second time the ball is hit on one side of the net, and it prepares for the third and final touch of the ball. This third hit must be over the net into the opposing team's court. You usually want to try for a spike on the third hit.

To set up for a spike, pass the ball on a high arc and sail it near the net on your side of the court. The ball must end up in a good position for the spiker to jump up and smash it.

THE SET

Eyes On The Ball

Fingers Spread

Elbows Out

Make Contact With Ball In Front Of Face

Knees Bent

Feet Spread

Regular Overhand Pass To Spot Near Net

Straighten Knees

Keep Feet On Floor—Don't Jump

To make a set, stand with your feet spread. Your weight should be on the balls of your feet. Keep your knees flexed.

As the ball comes toward you, make contact with it just in front of your face. The pass itself is done exactly like a regular overhand pass (see page 49). The big difference, however, is that you are passing to a spot rather than to another player. In a set, you send the ball to a specific area near the net where it can be spiked by one of your teammates.

As you make the set, straighten your flexed knees so you get your body into the pass. But don't try to jump as you set the ball. Just try to make your set so that the ball is about five or six feet above the net and about three feet away from the net on your side.

RUNNING A BASIC VOLLEYBALL PLAY

Volleyball is a team sport. Team play means passing and setting up for other players. In general, players in the back row try to get the ball to the front row. Players in the front row try to set up each other for a spike or dink. (See pages 42-46.)

In volleyball, the player who first receives or touches a ball hit over the net from the opposing team's side becomes the *passer.* A passer's job is to prevent an inbounds ball from touching the floor and also to reduce the ball's speed and spin. While doing that, the passer sends the ball over to the *setter.* A setter's job is to pass the ball in such a way that a teammate can easily spike it. Basically, that's how all volleyball plays are run: pass, set, then spike (or dink).

TYPICAL VOLLEYBALL PLAY

1. Pass   2. Setup   3. Spike

DIGGING THE BALL

A two-handed dig is the same as an underhand return (see page 40). In this instance, however, your goal is to direct the ball to one of your teammates rather than to send it back over the net.

The chief problem with the two-handed dig is being in the correct position to dig the ball. It's also especially hard for beginners to get a dig to go just where they want it to go.

Sometimes you have to keep the ball from hitting the floor any way you can. One advanced technique you can learn to keep the ball off the floor and in play is a one-hand dig pass. It is used to save a low shot or a shot to the extreme right or left of you. It can be done with either hand.

TWO-HAND DIG PASS

Ball Hits Here

First, stretch your hitting hand out palm up and away from your body. Now curl your fingers into a fist and close your thumb over them. You will use your fist and the heel of your hand to hit the ball in a one-hand dig.

To make a one-hand dig pass, you'll have to be in a crouched position low to the floor. Start your arm swing about even with your side. Do not draw your arm too far back. Bring your extended arm forward to meet the ball as it comes toward you. Make sure to keep your eyes on the ball. You want to hit it dead center under the ball, not off to one side or the other. Snap your wrist as you stroke the ball upward.

ONE-HAND DIG PASS

Body Low

Arm Swing
Starts Even
With Side

Eyes On Ball

Bring
Arm
Forward

Hit Ball
On Bottom
With Fist

Snap
Wrist

UNDERHAND PASS

Little Or No
Upward Swing

Keep
Hands
Low

Bend
Knees

Bat Ball
Quickly

Palms Up

Thumbs
Out

UNDERHAND PASS

To make an underhand pass, turn both your hands so that the palms face skyward. Hold your hands just about waist high. They should be spaced apart so that your outstretched pinky fingers cannot touch.

As the ball comes toward you, bend your knees and keep your hands low. Your wrists and fingers should be rigid as you swing your hands up to meet the ball. The idea is to hit the ball quickly upward the instant it touches your hands. To prevent a carry, immediately halt the upward motion of your arm swing as soon as you hit the ball with your hands.

The underhand pass is a two-handed hit that is often used in *un*official volleyball games. But it is illegal in official volleyball games and tournaments. That's because the underhand pass frequently results in holding or carrying the ball, which is against the rules. Use the underhand pass only when you have no other alternative. And in official games, avoid it.

NET SAVE

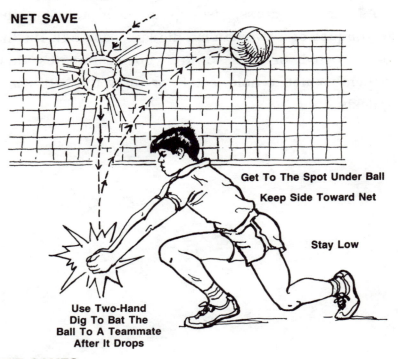

Get To The Spot Under Ball

Keep Side Toward Net

Stay Low

Use Two-Hand Dig To Bat The Ball To A Teammate After It Drops

NET SAVES

Sometimes, a player on your team may hit the ball into the net during a game. Just because the ball is hit into the net does not mean you automatically have to give up a point or side out. The ball can be saved or legally played off the net as long as you don't touch the net. That is called a net save.

Since a volleyball net has some play in it, the ball may stick or hang against the net for a second or so before dropping. That will give you time to get into position to play the ball. Get to a spot under the ball quickly. Keep your knees bent and have your side to the net. Be careful not to go under the net into the opposing team's court. That's illegal.

As the ball drops, rise up to meet it, using the techniques of a two-handed dig (see page 54). Hit the ball up high or back toward your teammates. Just remember not to hold, catch, or carry the ball. Hit it quickly.

Other Forms of Volleyball

Volleyball is a game that can be adapted to suit just about any number of players. The following are some forms of volleyball that are very popular in many places.

BEACH VOLLEYBALL

Beach volleyball, a game mostly played outdoors on the beach, has just two players on each team. That's why it's sometimes called *two-player volleyball.* In this game, the playing area is reduced. The court measures twenty feet wide and forty feet long.

BEACH VOLLEYBALL

As usual, only a serving team can score points. But it takes only eleven points to win a beach volleyball game. All the other scoring rules are the same as regular volleyball.

The two players on each side position themselves so that one is in the front and the other is in the back. They take turns serving after side outs. As in regular volleyball, each side is allowed just three hits.

There's a lot of ground to cover in beach volleyball, a fast-paced game. It's often played in the hot summer sun by or near oceans and lakes. Have fun playing it. But don't push yourself too hard, and protect yourself from too much sun.

WALLEYBALL

This unofficial volleyball game is played on an inside court that is smaller than regulation size and has no boundaries. Many walleyball players use a racquetball court.

Shots can be played or hit off the side or back walls. (That's how the name "walleyball" started.) Points are scored only if the ball touches the floor. Other than that, all regular volleyball rules apply.

UNLIMITED-HIT VOLLEYBALL

In this form of volleyball, all the regular rules apply except the number of players on a team and the number of hits each side is allowed on any given play. There are no restrictions on the size of a team or how many times a team can hit the ball before returning it over the net. Points are scored if the ball touches the floor or is hit out of bounds.

Great Fun, Great Exercise

It really doesn't matter what form of volleyball you play or at what level of competition. It can be a friendly game on a beach, in the back yard, or in a gym. It can also be an intense match in an official tournament. What's important is that you *enjoy* playing it.

Great fun and great exercise—that's volleyball. And now that you know how to play it, what are you waiting for? Round up your friends and head for the volleyball court!

INDEX